Arrighi's Running Hand

Arrighi's Running Hand

A Study of Chancery Cursive

Including a Facsimile of the
1522 "Operina"
with side by side translation

& an Explanatory Supplement

to help Beginners
in the Italic Hand by

Paul Standard

A Pentalic Book
Taplinger Publishing Company
New York

First Edition
First published in the United States in 1979 by
Taplinger Publishing Co., Inc., New York, N.Y.

Copyright © 1979 by Paul Standard
All rights reserved. Printed in the U.S.A.

Facsimile of Arrighi's "Operina" courtesy
John M. Wing Foundation, The Newberry Library, Chicago

LC Number: 78-58412
ISBN 0-8008-0323-X (cloth)
ISBN 0-8008-0324-8 (pbk)

Dedicated
to Stella,
& to my Students &
Colleagues,

all comprising a Legion
of fellow-Pioneers in
Chancery Cursive's
Revival.

To the memory of my friend
George Salter
whose grasp of every phase
of a book's making
has been a continuing inspiration;

& to his brilliant pupil
Philip Grushkin
whose constant advice has helped
bring this book to its completion,

I make grateful
Acknowledgment.

J.S.

Contents

Introduction

Long considered the finest writing manual of the western world, Ludovico degli Arrighi's _La Operina_ remains an ideal text for all wish to recapture what we are still in some danger of losing—a running hand at once clear, graceful & self-respecting. Chancery Cursive script may seem beyond the layman's power to acquire, and yet it is far less difficult than the scripts used since the United States achieved nationhood. I say less difficult when I really believe it to be easy; easy by reason of its built-in logic and by the use of an ideal instrument, the edged pen—its working edge beveled as in a chisel. This tool, virtually forgotten in the world's schoolrooms these four centuries past, has by its recent rediscovery now become the secret weapon of handwriting reform on both sides of the Atlantic.

This edged pen (I think of it as a miniature screw-driver's edge) replaces the pointed or the ball-pointed pencil (each of the last two resembling the end of an ice-pick). Our sketch will show how the pseudo-ice-pick, dipped in ink, gives a wavy line of unvarying thinness, like a thread laid on paper; whereas the pseudo-screw-driver's effort yields an undulating ribbon of graduated thicks and thins, their variance depending on the direction of the stroke. It is this variety that fascinates and inspires every beginner—child & adult alike. For italic script the pen is held so that its sidling stroke (its thinnest) is about 45° to the horizontal line of writing, thus adding flesh & blood to every letter's shape; in contrast, the pointed pen is limited to anæmic skeleton forms.

Now more than 2,000 years old, the edged pen has been hailed by the late Edward Johnston, the father of modern calligraphy, as "the supreme letter-making tool"—the instrument that created the Greek, the Hebrew, the Arabic & the Latin scripts, as well as their variants. Accordingly the reader may now be willing to accept a modest revision in my opening paragraph, where I described the change to italic as something merely 'less difficult'. But my experience in converting a number of private schools to italic convinces me that the restored tool has made that change both easy and natural.

We may be ready to rank the Operina as the first & finest manual. But it remains a small book of only 32 pages, which may be right for a pioneering work. Its entire text was cut in reverse on woodblocks whose inked surfaces produced a volume now as rare as it is famous. Arrighi's object was to teach the Chancery Cursive letters for the first time by means of a printed manual. An earlier attempt by Sigismondo Fanti to show this alphabet in 1514 had failed for lack of a craftsman able to cut those slim letters in wood. By 1522 Arrighi was luckier; he had found in Ugo da Carpi the very man for the job, & the Operina duly appeared that year—but with a preface confessing that "the press cannot entirely represent the living hand." Perhaps he should have explained that even Da Carpi could not give each letter its narrow (but not pointed) hairpin turns, nor could his cutting-medium do more than approximate the pen forms the author had written out for him. Beyond this, the imprinted images further distorted those which the scribe had lightly put onto his original paper. Arrighi's cautionary phrase, then, is what would be expected from his close knowledge of printing & from his own experience in designing types; yet he evidently felt that printed images of his writing would serve the beginner.

Of Arrighi himself we have no record after the year 1527, and yet his name is oftener uttered in gratitude than that of any of his contemporaries. He lives mainly by his own works – works which came to life again half a century ago, when the late Stanley Morison's devoted research re-presented Arrighi to the small but growing band of aspiring scribes & typophiles of the western world. From Morison's book we learn that Arrighi was born in Vicenza, as his Latin appellatives — 'Vicentinus' & 'Vicentino' – amply confirm. Beginning professional life as a teacher of writing in Venice, he went on to Rome and found a place in the college of writers of apostolic briefs for the Vatican. Thus far, no research of the Vatican archives has turned up any example of his work as a scribe. Yet the very title of his 1522 Operina calls him a 'scrittore de brevi apostolici', which leaves no doubt of his

Vatican connection. In 1523 his concern with letterforms extended) to the design of italic printing types, of which he produced three in the next few years. His was the earliest use of a calligraphic italic type in the preface of his own supplemental study, Il Modo de Temperare (1523), which explains the method of cutting a quill pen, & then goes on to show a dozen styles of text and decorative letters for the use of other craftsmen.

Latter-day disciples of italic writing remain grateful for Arrighi's manual, but they keep wishing he had left us a sequel to the Operina—a sequel showing all continuing students how set-hand characters can be ideally strung out with those joins that will make a running hand—the one thing his manual's subtitle declares to be his purpose. All who have seen reproduced pages from Arrighi's manuscripts may still hope that some scrap of his informal writing would (as some day it may) somehow turn up. Until then we shall not fully know what miracles that disciplined hand was capable of.

Arrighi's manual was an instant success; its methods were widely copied in neighboring countries until almost the end of the 1500's. From then, writing manuals proliferated all over Europe, but the Operina was forgotten until the first facsimile appeared in 1926, carrying the first study of Arrighi's work both as calligrapher and type designer. Its longish title is: "The Calligraphic Models of Ludovico degli Arrighi surnamed Vicentino / A Complete Facsimile and Introduction by Stanley Morison / Paris · Privately Printed for Frederic Warde · Mcmxxvj." Its colophon reads: "For and under the direction of Frederic Warde & with his Arrighi types three hundred copies of this book have been privately printed on the hand-presses of the Officina Bodoni at Montagnola di Lugano, Switzerland· March Mcmxxvi." It was printed by the late Dr. Giovanni Mardersteig, whose death at 85 in Verona in 1977 brought world-wide tributes ranking him as the greatest & perhaps the last hand-press master-printer of our time. Indeed, in linking the names Mardersteig-Morison-Warde we have a fortunate trio of friends whose mutual interest in letterforms, typography and calligraphy made them famous in the worlds of fine bookmaking & of handwriting generally. All three were admirers & practitioners of italic; and Warde's handwriting may well be the earliest and is certainly the best example of the revived Chancery Cursive at its most austere and its most humane.

My chief aim in the ensuing pages is to help the beginner in acquiring a good italic hand by an analysis of the small letters and a showing of how the italic caps differ (while yet deriving) from such forms as are given chiefly by the Trajan inscription. Additional diagrams will explain points of variance which can then be judged objectively, always mindful of the need to avoid clutter & prettification.

We all want a handwriting that will retain clarity, vigor & grace even when written at speed. But as speed is hard to define, let me suggest rhythm rather than speed as an ideal. No hand written at breakneck speed can avoid producing a jumbled scrawl. My speed may not be yours, but we can agree on a certain rhythm that will set down a series of sentences as easily read as written – written after learning the letter shapes; for then only is the hand 'commanded' by a memory already trained for every emergent shape.

It is worth recalling that Elder Brewster, the only member of the Pilgrim band with a university background, was the first of the Mayflower passengers to write the italic hand he had picked up while at Cambridge; and that William Bradford, the second governor of Massachusetts Bay Colony, wrote his account of the Plymouth Plantation in a clear italic. Aside from these two Pilgrim Fathers, all other arriving Pilgrims brought with them the English round hand, or its continental varieties. These simply became acclimated to New World uses, and so continued into the 1880's, when the infant typewriter entered the business world. The pen, though mightier than the sword, could not compete in speed against the machine. The time seemed exactly right for some perceptive educationist to suggest a twofold decision: ① to let the typewriter & related machines assume the drudgeries of business, and ② to let the hand recapture for handwriting those very qualities so long sacrificed for the sake of business. Had this country then possessed a scholar learned in handwriting's history, the liberating italic script might, a full century earlier, have brought back the tool which during two millenia had formed the Hebrew, Greek, Latin & Arabic alphabets.

Another irony, more recent, emerges from the handwriting 'reform' movement of the 1920's, when certain private schools adopted some hands known as manuscript writing, print script, book hand and the like. All these scripts were well-meaning, and all mistaken only because all were based on roman characters. As these are not equipped for joining, they all suppressed the running quality of most earlier hands. Had the italic hand been chosen, this running quality would have persisted, as in any truly cursive script. The reformers, however, resisted this simple truth; they regarded joinability as an impediment to fluency, 'true speed' coming, in their view, from the increased number of stops their scripts required! Yet this balked 'reform' did bring us one inadvertent benefit; it reintroduced the edged pen, & thus restored the historic instrument which had long since established its primacy and utility in all western scripts.

Leafing through the Operina, the reader sees that of its 32 pages only 19 (4 through 22) are strictly instructional; and these give the full details needed for the small letters—heights, breadths, spacing & joins. But the capitals & their variants, plus the ampersand, suddenly appear together on page 22 without preparation by any showing of the simpler romans from which they derive. Such a showing, offered in the addendum, can be revealing to the beginner, with whom I later share something of what my years of teaching the edged pen's use have taught me about the italic family.

With this tool in hand, the italic forms are so readily acquired that all objection is now subdued and the future of italic seems assured. In the ensuing facsimile I have set my English versions always alongside the original Italian, correcting some past misapprehensions & clarifying some hitherto neglected passages whose logic is now restored in a few fortunate break-throughs, which my earliest classroom charts now show to be in strict accord with Arrighi's intentions. Beyond the facsimile (but keyed to its pages) I have placed my addenda. These include a study of the capitals derived from the clearest historic forms, along with a study of Arabic numerals and extras not treated in the manual. All these may aid in restoring to Chancery Cursive its pristine eminence & utility. Handwriting was long considered Everyman's handicraft—a ranking that Arrighi's now revived genius can still help young or old aspirants to regain.

LA OPERINA

di Ludouico Vicentino, da

imparare di

scriue=

re

littera Can=

cellares=

cha

La Operina

of Ludovico Vicentino,
for learning to write
the Chancery letter

(1)

The Method & Rule
for Writing the Cursive
or Chancery letter
newly composed by
Ludovico Vicentino
Writer of Apostolic Briefs.
Rome, in the Year of
our Salvation
1522

IL MODO
&
Regola de' scriuere' littera
corsiua
ouer Cancellarescha
nouamente' compos̄to per
LVDOVICO
VICENTI=
NO
Scrittore' de' breui
aplici
in Roma nel Anno di n̄ra
Salute'
+ MDXXII +

A

Al benigno Lettore :~

Pregato piu uolte, anzi constretto da molti amici
benignissimo Lettore, che riguardo hauendo alla publica utilita e comodo non solamente di
questa eta, ma delli posteri anchora, uolessi
dar qualche essempio di scriuere, et regulata-
mente formare gli caratteri e note delle lre (
che cancellaresche hoggi di chiamano) uolétier
pigliai questa fatica: E perche impossibile era
de mia mano porger tanti essempi, che sodissfa-
cessino a tutti, mi sono ingegnato di ritrouare
questa nuoua inuentione de lre, e metterle in
stampa, le quali tanto se auicinano alle scritte a mano, quanto capeua il mio ingegno, E se
puntualmente in tutto no te rispondono, sup-
plicoti che mi facci iscusato, Conciosia che la
stampa no possa in tutto ripresentarte la vi-
ua mano, Spero nondimeno che imitando tu
il mio ricordo, da te stesso potrai consequire il
tuo desiderio . Uiui, e Sta Sano :~

To the gracious Reader

Entreated, indeed compelled by many
friends, most gracious Reader, out of
regard for the public need and convenience
not only of this age but of posterity as well,
to give some examples of the writing &
regular formation of the letters now called
Chancery, I gladly undertake this task.
ET since I could not offer enough examples of
my own hand to satisfy all, I have used this new
invention of letters & put them into print,
& they come as close to my handwriting as I can
manage. If they do not answer all your needs,
I pray you pardon me, since the preß cannot
fully represent the living hand. Yet I hope that
by following my teaching you will achieve
your desire. Long life, ET good Health :~

(3)

Whoever would learn to write the
running or Chancery letter
should observe the norms
shown below, &
First should learn to make
these two strokes: -/,
with one of which all
the Chancery letters
begin.
Of these two, the one
is flat & thick,
and the other
is slanting & thin,
as you can see:

-/-/-

—

A chiunq; uole' imparare' scriuere' lra
corsiua, o sia Cancellaresca conuiene'
osseruare' la sottoscritta norma
&
Primieramente' imparerai di fare' que=
sti dui' tratti', cioe - ´
da li quali se' principiano tutte'
le'
littere' cancellare=
sche;
Deli quali dui tratti l'uno é piano et
grosso,
l'altro é' acuto et sotti
le'
come' qui tu puoi uedere' notato

· ´ - ´ ·

-

Dal

primo adunq̃

Tratto piano ẽ gros=

so cioe' - - - che' alla riuersa

ẽ tornando per il medesmo se' incom:

mincia,

principiarai tutte' le' infrascritte' littere'

-a b c d f g h k l o g s ſ x

x y z

Lo resto poi' delo Alphabeto se' principia

dalo

Secundo Tratto acuto

ẽ Sottile' con il taglio dela penna ascé=

dendo et poi

allo ingui

Ritornando in questo modo designato

ı e e' i m n p r t u ÿ ·

First do

the flat ẽ thick

Stroke ⁓, with which, reversed

ẽ turning upon itself [⁓ca], you

begin all the following letters

·a b c d f g h h k l o g ſ x

x y z

The rest of the Alphabet begins

with the second Stroke,

slanting ẽ thin,

rising with the pen's edge

and then

Returning downwards as shown·

ıⅽ+⁓=e e' i m n p r t u ÿ /

(5)

From the first stroke, thick & flat,

make this body o⎺c o,

whence come five letters

a d c g g

Their bodies, all touching

the line on which

you will write,

must each

be formed not within

a perfect square, but rather

within

a sloping oblong,

in this way:

□ ⸗ ⸗ ⸗ ᴃ ᴀ ᴄ ᴄ d g ⸬ g □

a d c g g

Farai dal primo tratto groſſo &⸗ pia=
no queſto corpo o ⎺ r o dal
quale ne caui poi cinque littere

a d c g g

Dele quali lře tutti li corpi che toca=
no la linea ſopra

la quale tu ſcri

uerai,

ſe hanno

da

formare

in

vno quadreto oblongo

et

non quadro perfet to, in tal modo

cioe □ ⸗ ⸗ ᴃ ᴀ ᴄ ᴄ d g ⸬ g □

a d c g g

Vltra le' retro=
scritte' cinque' littere' a c d g g
ti fo intendere'
che' anchora quasi tutte' le' altre' lre'
se' hanno á formare' in questo :: qua=
dretto oblungo et non quadro per
fetto □
perche' al'occhio mio la littera
corsiua ouero Cancellarescha
vuole hauere'
del
lungo & non del rotondo: che' rotonda
ti veneria fatta qua=
do dal quadro
perfetto
& non oblungo la formasti

Besides
the above five letters
a c d g g,
you are to understand that
almost all the other letters are
formed within this sloping oblong ::,
and not within
a perfect square □;
because to my eye the cursive
or Chancery letter
wants to be long & not round:
and round is all it could be
if shaped within
an upright square
& not in a sloping oblong.

In alphabetical order, then, you will
learn to make this opening line ſ,
with the first thick and flat stroke
ˉſ ˉſ
whence you will develop
the following letters
b d ff f b k lſſ ſf l bll lb ſl
& to do them properly you will make
the top headstroke a bit thicker
than its descending stem
—a thickening easily made if you begin it
in reverse and retrace it backwards
over itself, then down to base, so: ˉˉſſ
ſbd fff b k llll bſſ ll ˉ

P_seguire' poi l'ordine' de' l'Alphabeto im=
parerai di fare' questa linea ſ principia=
dola con lo primo tratto groſſo et piano
ˉſ ˉſ
dala quale' ne' caueraï le' littere' in=
fraſcritte'
b d fff b k lſ ſſ ſſ l bll lbſl
& per fare' che habbiano la ragione' ſua
li' farai in cima quella te
ſtolina un poco piu groſſeta che' la linea,
La qual groſſeza tu facil=
—mente'farai
ſe' facendo il primo tratto lo comen=
ci alla riuerſa, & dapoi
ritorni indrieto per
lo medeſmo
ſbd fff bkllllb bſſll ˉ

Quando harai impa=
rato
di fare le
tre antescritte, quali tutte comin=
ciano da quel primo tratto grosso e
piano chio t'ho detto, te ne ve=
nerai ad quelle
che
con il secundo tratto acuto et sotti=
le se debbono principiare, come
seguendo in que=
sto mio
Trattatello facilmente potrai
da te
stesso
Comprende=
re

B

When you have learned
to make
the letters just written,
all beginning with that
thick & flat stroke,
you will come to those
that begin with the second
stroke slanting & thin,
which, by following this
little Treatise
of mine
you will by yourself
easily be able to
understand

(9)

The letters that begin with the
slanting & thin stroke
are these:
ıı e e' ij m n p r
t u
All these should be equal,
save that p and t should be
a little taller than the bodies of
the other letters
as shown by this example
apatmtumpnoturpgrstumputinatmpi
ET this greater height in the p
–of the rising line, not the loop–is in
my view more pleasing.
As to t, it is so made
to distinguish it from c.

Le littere' per tanto, quali dal secundo trat=
to acuto & sottile' se' princi=
piano, sonno le' infrascritte', Cioe'
ıı e e' ij m n p r
t u
le' quali tutte' deueno essere' eguali, saluo
che' il p et il t hanno da essere' un
poco piu altette' che' li corpi dele' altre'
tre'
come' quiui con lo exem
pio Ti dimostro
apatmtumpnoturpgrstumputinatmpi
ET questa piu alteza del p cioe' dela linea
et non dela panza, a l'occhio mio as=
sai piu satisface': Del t poi, si fa p farlo
differente' da vno, c.

Ma perche' hauemo due' sorte' di s ſ co=
me' uedi, & dela lunga te' ho insegnato,
Resta dire de'la piccola, de'la gua=
le' farai che'l uoltare'
di sotto sia
maggiore' che' quello
di sopra
si come' qui vedi signato
s s s
Incominzandola pure' con lo primo tra=
t to grosso e' piano ch'io
ti d'issi
& ritornando per lo medesmo idrieto
voltandolo al modo che'l sia vno
s
che s'intenda

But since we have two kinds of s ſ,
as you see, & as I have taught you
the long one, it remains
to speak of the smaller,
whose lower curve should be
greater than the upper, as here shown
· s s s ·
Beginning with the thick & flat
headstroke, as I have said,
return it back on itself
& write an opposed curve
so as to form an
s
as now understood

Coming to the xyz
we find x and y beginning
in almost the same way
thus: ʋ, crossing midway
of the first stroke to make the x,
whose front should be
no taller than an a.
Give the y the same depth
in this way:
xayaxayaxayaxy.
Of the z, then,
teach yourself to make it
with these strokes:

⌐7 Z 3 Z
ʒ ʒ Z
8

Auemo anchora da dire' de lo x y z
de le' quali tre' lre' lo x et y comincia=
no quasi ad uno modo
medesmo
cioé ʋ così, tagliando nel mezo de lo
primo tratto per fare' lo x, et che' dindri
non sia più largo che' quanto e' alto
vno a,
Lo simile' farai del y quanto a l'alteza,
in tal modo
xayaxayaxayaxy
De'
La z poi ti sforzera di far=
la con questi tratti che' qui sonno signati
⌐7 Z 3 Z
ʒ ʒ Z
8

Te bisogna poi imparato
l'Alphabeto, per congiungere' le' lr'e'
insieme' aduertire' che' tutte' le' haste' sia=
no eguali, come' sonno b d h k l
con lo suo puntcto icima
pendente' rotundo e grosetto in modo del
principio de uno c l L
Sinilmente' le' gambe' desotto
siano pari a una
mesura
f g p q s x y ss
& che li corpi de' tutte' le' liittere' ua=
dino eguali cosi disotto come' di sopra
in questo modo qui=
ui signato
A a b c d e m f n g m h i k l m n o p q r s t u s t u m v x y z

The Alphabet learned, we must
now, in putting the letters
together, see to it that all ascenders
be equal, as are b d h k l, with the
little top leaning forward,
rounded [repeat: rounded]
and thick,
like the beginning of c l l.
The descenders, too, should show
a common depth:
f g p q s x y ss
& the bodies of all the letters
should be even,
both below and above,
as here shown:
A a b c d e m f n g m h i k l m n o p q r s t u m v m x y z

(13)

ET as some letters of the Alphabet
are made in one stroke
without lifting pen from paper,
and some in two strokes,
it seems proper
to say just which are made
in one stroke, &
which in two.
Those that are made in
a single   stroke
are the   following:
abcghiklImnogrsſuy&z
The remaining letters
are each made in two strokes:
d e e' f k p t x & ʃ

Et perche' de' tutte' le' littere' de' lo
Alphabeto, alcune' se' fanno in uno
tratto senza leuare'
la penna desopra la carta, alcune' in
dui tratti
Mi e' parso al proposito dirti, quali
sonno quelle' che' con vno, quali gl=
le' che' con dui tratti se' facciano,
Quelle' che' con vno
tratto   se' fanno,
sonno le'   infrascrit=
te. cioe
abcghilImnogrsſuyz
Lo resto poi de' l'Alphabe
to
Se' fa in dui Tratti
d e e' f k p t x &

(14)

Saperai anchora Lettor mio che dele
littere piccole delo Alphabeto,
alcune si ponno ligare con le sue seguen
ti, et alcune no: Quelle che si
ponno ligare con le seguenti, sonno le
infrascritte, cioe, a c d f i k l m
n ſ s t u
Dele quali a d i k l m n u si ligano
con tutte le seguenti: Ma c f ſ s t ligano sol con alcune: Lo resto poi delo
Alphabeto cioe b e e g h o p g r x y z
non se deue ligar mai con lra
seguente. Ma nel liga
re, et non ligare ti
lascio in arbitrio
tuo, purche la
littera sia e-
guale.

You should, my Reader, also know that
of the small letters of the Alphabet
some may be joined to those that follow,
& some not. Those that may be so joined are
a c d f i k l m n ſ s t u
Of which the a d i k l m n u are joined to
all followers: But c f ſ s t join only
to some. The rest of the Alphabet,
that is, b e e g h o p g r x y z
ought never to join any follower.
But whether to join
or not to join I leave to
your judgment
provided that
the letters be
equal.

(15)

Here follows an example of the letters
joinable to any that follow:
aa ab ac ad ae' af ag ah ai ak al am an
ao ap aq ar as af at au ax ay az
The like may be done with d i k l m n u.
The joins for c f s ſ t follow:
ct, fa ff fi fm fn fo fr fu fy,
ſt st
ſf ſſ ß ſt, ta te' ti tm tn to tq tr tt tu
tx ty
The remaining letters of the Alphabet,
Namely b e' g h o p q r x y z 3
should not be joined to
any following letter.

Seguita lo eſſempio delle' lre' che pono
ligarſi con tutte'le' ſue ſeguenti, in tal mo
do Cioe'
aa ab ac ad ae' af ag ah ai ak al am an
ao ap aq ar as af at au ax ay az
Il medeſmo farai con d i k l m n u.
Le ligature' poi de' c f s ſ t ſonno
le' infra =
ſcritte
ct, fa ff fi fm fn fo fr fu fy,
ſt st
ſf ſſ ß ſt, ta te' ti tm tn to tq tr tt tu
tx ty
Con le reſtanti littere' de'lo Alphabeto, che'
ſono, b e' g h o p q r x y z 3
non ſi deue' ligar mai lra
alcuna ſequente'

(16)

Acciò che' nel scriuer tuo Tu habbi
piu facilita, farai che'
tutti li
caraltheri, o uogli dire' littere
pendano inanzi, ad
questo modo
Cioe'

Virtus omnibus rebus anteit profelto :~

Non uoglio però che' caschino tanto Ma
cosi feci l'essempio, per
dimostrarti meglio la via doue' dilfe
littere'
hanno da stare'
pendenti.,

C

To gain facility in your writing,
let all your small letters
slope slightly forward
[as do all herein, save for
the ensuing Latin sentence].

Virtus omnibus anteit profectus.

The foregoing line
is offered as a contrasting example,
so that you may, instead,
follow the moderate normal slope
used throughout
this book.

(17)

Though I have told you, gracious Reader,
that all the characters slope forward,
I would have you understand
this to apply only to the small letters
&
I would have your Capitals always
written upright,
&
with their strokes firm and
showing no inner tremors
since otherwise, in my view,
they will be lacking in
Grace.

Nota, gratioso Lettor mio, che' quatunq3
ti habbia ditto, che' tutti li
caratheri deueno esser pendenti inanzi,
voglio che' tu intendi questo
quanto alle lre' piccole,

Z
voglio ch' le' tue' Maiuscule' sempre'
siano tirate' drite'
&
con li suoi tratti fermi e'
saldi senza tremoli per dentro, che'
altramente', a mio parer

non
haueriano Gra
tia
Alcuna

Farai che la
distantia
da linea a linea de cose che tu
scriuerai in tal littera
Cancellaresca
non sia troppo larga, ne troppo stretta, ma
mediocre
Et la distantia da parola á parola sia
quanto e vno n: Da littera ad
littera poi nel ligarle sia
quanto é il biancho tra le due gambe
de lo n
Ma perche seria quasi impossibile serua=
re questa regola, te sforzarai di consigliar=
ti con l'occhio, et á quello satisfare, il
quale ti scusara bonissi
mo Compasso

Make sure that the distance
between lines of whatever you write
in this Chancery letter
ought not to be too large or too small,
but moderate,
& the space from word to word equal
to the width of an n; & from letter
to letter within a word
leave as much white as within
the legs of an n.
But if you find it impossible
to keep this rule, try to
let your eye be the judge & so
resolve your difficulty.

Enough having been shown
of my way of writing the
Chancery hand's small letters,
it now remains to speak
of the Capitals.
All these ought to begin
with the two strokes used in
the small letters —
the one flat & thick,
the other slanting & thin
in
this
way
-/-/-/

Credo assai á bastanza hauerti dimostrato
il modo del mio scriuere littera
Cancellarescha, quanto alle lre piccole :
Hora ci resta da dirti p
quanto alle Maiuscu=
le si pertenga ,
le quali tutte se deueno principiare
da quelli dui tratti ch'io t'ho detto de
le piccole cioe l'uno piano et grosso, l'al=
tro acuto, e sottile
in
tal
modo
-/-/-/-

Graue fatica non ti fia ad imparar fare le
littere Maiuscule, quando nelle pic=
cole harai firmato bene
la mano, et
eo maxime ch'io ti ho
ditto che li Dui principij delle
Piccole sonno anchora quelli delle Grandi
come continuando il scriuere, da te
medesimo uenerai
cognoscendo
Non ti diro adunque altro, Saluo che te
Sforzi imparar fare le tue Maiuscule
Come qui apresso ri=
trouerai per esse=
pio designato

It should not be hard for you
to learn to write Capitals, since
your hand has gained sureness
with the Smalls. And chiefly
I should tell you that the two main
strokes of the Smalls
apply also to the Capitals,
as, by continuing to write,
you will by yourself
come to know.
Nothing else needs saying, save
that you should
now learn to make the Capitals
as written for you
in the following
examples.

[Operina's instructional text
having ended overleaf,
Arrighi uses
the remaining pages for a series
of moral & ethical maxims
to 'train the hand'
and to present variant models
for capitals & for
incidental decoration, so that
the beginner's taste
may be formed from the quoted
examples.]

AA ABC CDD E CFF
GGH HJKKLLMM
MMN NOOTPPQ
RRSSTTJVUVV
XXYYZ ZQ & &cet

~: Ludouicus Vicentiℕ. ſcribebat :~
+ Rome anno domini +
• MDXXII •

A abcdemfmgmhiklmmopqrſtumxmxyz.
• ℃·

~: Exempli per firmar la Mano :~

A·r o a b c o d i e e' f o g h i k l m n o p q p g
o r s ſ t u x y y z̄, ɛт ſt ſſ ſſ ſß ſtu vo W

No é Gloria il principio, ma il seguire'. De'
gui naſce' l'honor uero. &
perfecto:
Che' vale' in campo intrare', et poi fuggire'?

Ille' Idem. L. Vicentinus Scribebat Rome'.

I The student will be well advised
to proceed
from the given quotations
to others he will have
treasured up in other languages
using our alphabet.
He will thus form
his own 'golden treasury'
for the design of pages
wherein
decoration is so tempered
by modesty
as never to dominate
the text. I

(23)

A -: Deo optimo & Immortali auspice :-

A a b c d e e f g g h i k l m n o p q r s s t u x x
x y x y z z e e & I

Cosi ua il stato human: Chi questa sera Finisce
il corso suo, Chi diman nasce. Sol
virtu doma Morte horrida
, e, altera .

Ludo . Vice tinus Rome in Parhione
Scribeba .

· A N N · M D X X I I ·

Deo , & Virtuti omnia debent ,

(24)

ABCDEFGHIKLMM
NOPQRSTVXYZZ

abcdeefgghiklmnopqrsstux
xyzzeʒ &

Est modus in rebus : sunt
certi
deniqʒ fines
Quos vltra citraqʒ nequit consistere
Rectum

AABCDEFGHIKLMNOPQ
RSTVXYZ

Medium tenuere Beati

D

(25)

Aabbcdde Eff GghhijkKll
Mmnnopfqerr stuvvxxyz
zzfqerr

Fient autem commode omnia, si recte tempora
dispensabitur: Si singulis diebus statutas
horas litteris dabimus, neq
negocio vllo
abstrahamur; quo minus aliquid
quotidie legamus ..

Eodem Ludo. Vicentino scribete.VII. augu

In alma Vrbe

(26)

F . Petrar. dic

Segui gia le speranze, el van desio: Hor
ho dinanci agliocchi un chiaro specchio
Dou io veggio me stesso
el fallir
mio.
Et quanto posso al fine m'apparecchio,
Pensando
al
breue viuer mio nel quale
Sta mane era un fanciullo, & hor
son
vecchio :~

Breue & irreparabile Tempus

(27)

Reginam illam procacium uitiorꝝ Auaritiã
fugeʾ,
cui cuncta crimina detestabili deuotioneʾ
famulantur,
Queʾ quidem Auari=
tia
studium pecunieʾ habet, quam nemo sa=
piens concupiuit : Ea quasi malis ve=
nenis imbuta, corpus animumꝗꝫ
virilem effœmi=
nat

neꝗꝫ copia neꝗꝫ inopia minuitur

Auarus i nullo bonus i se aut peßimus :~

Hoc excellentis est sapien=
tiæ
hominem sui ipsius habere notitiam,
nec ex dilectione, quam habet in se=
ipso falla
tur
Et bonum se repute, cum non sit.
Dictabat hoc Galenus: Scribebat
Vicentinus i

VRBE
Potens quippe est homo suos quosqz
altius dirige=
re
seipsum si agnoue=
rit.

AVREA SENTENTIA

(29)

Amant.mo .A. Beat.mo Car.o Car.mo Char.mo

Dign.mo .Ex.mo .Exij. R. Pn. Famos.mo

Gnoso. A Lon Hon.mo Hon.lllmo lll.mo

lll.s . lll. lll.z . lll.880 . lll.mo K.co .

lL. M. Mag.tas Mag.tia Mag.co Nobil.mo O

Rincipi Pres.to R. R.mo Reueren

Ser.mo San.tas T.T Veniz.us Vra X.mo

yz

.Lud. Vicentin. Scribebat.

(30)

Lettor, se' truoui cosa che
　　t'offenda
In questo Trattatel del Vicenti:
　　no,
Non te' marauigliar, Perche' diui:
　　no,
Et non humano, é quel, ch' é senza,
　　menda.

Qui viuer non si puo senza
　　defetto
Che' chi potesse' Star senza pec:
　　cato
Seria simil á Dio
　　ch' é sol perfetto

The end of
the
Art
of
writing the Cursive
or Chancery letter
Printed in Rome from the original
of Ludovico Vicentino,
Writer

Finisce
la
ARTE
di
scriuere littera Corsiua
ouer Cancellares=
cha
Stampata in Roma, per inuentione
di Ludouico Vicentino,
scrittore

CVM GRATIA PRIVILEGIO

Preamble to
An Explanatory Supplement.

It has now become clear that Arrighi had reservations as to the quality of the script reproduced in his <u>Operina</u>, and we know his reason why. Hence every fresh facsimile of his manual owes its readers some clarification of critical points — a task, alas! to which only an Arrighi could do full justice. My comments are thus offered in all submission to that master. And I must still beg my gracious reader's indulgence for my suggestions, though they proceed from a long teaching experience.

My translations, confined to his 23 pages of instructional text, are set alongside his Italian. This means that his nine concluding pages (consisting of exemplary quotations) are left untranslated in their original Latin or Italian. They serve, as he intended, 'for training the hand' by practice with poetry or with golden sentiments in prose, which the student may transcribe; or, better still, replace with comparable passages treasured from Latin, Italian, English, French or German texts, to test his own proficiency. In this present section I shall key my suggestions to the <u>Operina's</u> numbered pages. Then, by discussion & detailed examples, I shall try to show what merits my alternatives may have.

33

Apart from the shaping of letters, I frequently show a way to avoid the needless heavying-up of a script, chiefly by introducing light without altering a letter's essential shape. The darkness is dispelled by replacing an ink-flooded contact with a tiny air-space of pseudo-contact — whereby a whole group of smalls and capitals regain a balanced texture.

A word about slope may be useful here. A universal rule in writing requires every national hand to slope in the direction of reading. This means that most western scripts (i.e., English, French, German, Greek, Italian, Russian, Spanish, Swedish) lean, as they read, to the right; and most near-eastern hands (Hebrew, Arabic, &c.) slope, as they read, to the left. Far-eastern scripts (such as Chinese, Japanese) have no lateral slope; all are written downward in vertical columns, starting at top-right & proceeding column-wise leftward; no ideogram shows any body-slope, each figure in the parallel rows hanging in balance as on an invisible vertical string. In our Chancery Italic writing, the letters duly slope some 5° forward. This is a concession to human frailty, since no hand can hope to write all small characters as pure verticals. But in the dawn of the printed letter G·B·Castiglione (in Milan, 1541) issued an italic type upright for caps & smalls alike — alike save in the few instances where they defeated the vigilance of the practised type-cutter. And on the imprinted page the recurring Johnny-out-of-step sloping character only too plainly declares its guilt to the reading eye. Such mishaps only confirm the

need for a slight forward slope in italic writing; for even if it slips from its 5°
to a mere 2° forward, it does still remain forward from the vertical, whereas
if it sloped only half a degree back of the vertical it would become one
more Johnny-out-of-step. Hence it is better to resist any script-vertical
requirement, even for caps alone. In many an early Aldine italic edition
such wayward caps tend to slip back of the vertical often enough to prove
how hard even a printing mechanism finds it to remain strictly vertical.

Our finest numerals, taken on permanent loan from the Arabs, are most
frequently disfigured by oversize extenders reaching a length equal to those
in our b d f g h l p q g y z. Such 'equal treatment' makes Arabics gawky &
unwieldy. They look their best in their native proportions, as some early
masters well realized—notably Ugo da Carpi, whose Thesauro de Scrittori
of 1535 shows eight striking pages of massed arabics in arithmetical uses.
But on this point Arrighi stands absolved; he used only roman numer=
als in his manual. We also promise a close study of the ampersand.

Enough of this for now. The point I offer is simply the need
to make the most of Chancery Cursive by learning first
to respect its forms, so that hand & eye & mind may
together teach us to discriminate
among emergent choices.

A Study of
Arrighi's Italic Characters

Because the edged pen is still so new to our generation, some diagrams
will help to clarify its powers and its needs. The words you are now reading,
being written with such a pen made of metal, show at once the nature of
the script. The edge held at 45° to the line writing, has a breadth of
about $\frac{1}{32}$", but occasional diagrams may be made with a wider edge
in a split pen or a double pencil, so as to expose details a beginner might
otherwise miss. But the rule for all such nibs is the same: the x-height
of our italic alphabet is 5 pen-widths, and extenders rise (or fall) by
another 5 units each.

The stray letters alongside
show how italic lines are

planned, with only 7¼ pen-widths allowed for caps, which thus have
come to be called 'subdued caps'.

A nib with edge cut square is used by right-handers, and by
most lefthanders as well; yet some few lefthanders may (I do not say must)
prefer an edge skewed (cut obliquely) to the left. Most right-handers
will naturally tilt slightly the paper's lower right corner some 15° or more

upward; the lefthander will instead tilt the left lower corner upward
by some 20° to 45°. The right-hander's cant of paper is relatively
slight because the square-cut nib *n* at once gives him his working position ⊏45°↓, whence proceed *uneo* & other
italic strokes. But the left-hander can gain a like position by
canting his sheet the other way, my *n* split-pen sketches showing Arrighi's *n*, which he calls 'la norma', as giving correct position
& proportion. Luckily, I early discovered a latent, if rudimentary,
capacity in my own left hand, & thus was enabled to teach more effect-
ively. In my classes I reserved ^my first private session for left-handers as a
group, my earlier demonstration having established that right-handers
could meanwhile proceed to their endeavors on their own. I would then
show the left-handers how to cope with their opening problem. They quickly
saw the logic of my procedure, which had incidentally exposed the oblique
nib's major fault – that its acute forward angle would plough into
the paper. This risk they preferred to avoid by using the square-cut nib.

    Writing in Arrighi's day was done with quill pens, and these still
remain the smoothest of writing tools; but as they are difficult to cut
or to sharpen to a matching width, the beginner will be wiser to rely
upon metal nibs. These are available in a full range of sizes, & the fountain
pen-with-broad nib is now a commonplace. When the student has come
to working terms with italic, his own manual responses will have taught

him or her to discriminate among writing tools.

For practice today the beginner should not disdain a paper merely because it is not handmade. Some machine-made papers are not only very good for writing but also very moderately priced. Costlier papers can wait until honored by the scripts they bear. Whatever the paper, it should not be laid on a glazed or polished surface, which will only impede the movements of your pen. Be sure to lay a sheet of blotting paper or a 3- or 4-ply blanket of soft paper (or even of imprinted newspaper) under your working sheet; you will feel its subtle invitation to clean work.

We know of course that the edged pen is its own measuring device, using its nib-width as guide to good letter proportions. Long scribal practice having established the ideal x-height at 5 nib-widths of the pen-in-hand, every change of pen will, by the like measurement, declare the new dimensions. In all such measuring (& only therein) the nib is held with its edge vertical, so that each unit is shown at the full linear width of the nib, which is cut square at its working end. Extenders are allowed a like 5 units (5 for ascenders & 5 for descenders), so that letter f can uniquely claim 15 units, which in practice is often moderated to perhaps 13, as will be seen in the examples. But when we write, rather than measure, our pen is constantly in 45° position, contributing substance to the letters, whereas the pointed pen yields only a pale monotony of hair-line.

We now proceed with our comments, stimulated by Arrighi's pages, each set within its own entablature:)   (.

) Page 4 (As your edged pen, always in 45° position, travels in practice strokes in every direction, you will sense why this pen steadily 'remembers' its function just where a beginner is apt to forget it, thus revealing a logical ribboned sequence of alternating thicks & thins, produced by a power no beginner ever dreamed of possessing or claiming. Introducing pen to pupil, Arrighi on this first instructional page says that all Chancery letters begin with one of two strokes — the one flat & thick ---, the other slanting & fine ///. His point becomes clearer, I think, in magnification -/-, -/-/-, ◢/◢/◢. The two latter sets of examples are made with nibs used in lettering rather than in writing, but their obedience to a common working rule reinforces the logic involved.

) Page 5 (Here we are shown how the opening thick stroke is made by starting towards the right for a very little way & then reversing & turning upon itself, begins virtually half the characters in the alphabet. We see, too, how the remaining letters all begin with the thin ascending stroke. To this latter group belong the xyz, which by some mischance have attached themselves to the flat-thick stroke group. Also, in the third-from-bottom line, the

40

block-cutter has given us a maverick word *ingiu*, which has lost a dot and a grave accent needed to make it read *ingiù*, meaning downward.

❡ In the first group (line 8), note that its ascenders all seem to have changed their promised flat-thick tops into arc-forms that henceforth become usual for them throughout the remaining text. Of the letters that follow, the archaic h has now passed out of use in favor of h, and we can allow the k to dispense with its needless base serif, & let its loop enter the cleared tail-stroke, thereby giving k more light within; and the ambiguous g, now commonly supplanted by a practical q that alternates with Q Q̣ or Q̣. Further, the b has gained a variant b with a bottom as in O, that will be useful when we come to joining letters. The e, made in two strokes, C + ? = e, needs two cautions: its bottom should be not angular but round, & its loop less than half of e's total height. So made, it readily joins *ea, ec, em, en, eo, ep, er,* &c., if we are careful to make the joining-stroke thin & oblique; an e with heavy horizontal ending is singularly aggressive at x-height's very middle, and should be avoided.

〔Page 5, continued〕 Let me confess that I have used Arrighi's phrase, 'flat & thick stroke' (*tratto piano e grosso*) with a mental reservation. For though his line 8 duly opens with a lone flat stroke in the sequence *-abcdfghklogsſx*, these alleged 'flats' become, as I have noted, shallow arcs not only on this line & page but all through the manual.

So I must suggest, in all submission, that 'flat & thick' is no more than an unhappy shorthand phrase, suited perhaps to a beginner's crude perception of the pen's modest role in putting down a little ink to start a shape. My double-pencil diagrams show that mere flatness can only rigidify the letters, whereas an arc vitalizes them. Starting with the flat top in two pairs of identical sequences, it is plain that ①, ② & ③ produce as little as they promise. The remaining, each with an arc-top, show at once what Arrighi surely had in mind and what his mss. confirm. It is the arc's thinning-out at its expiry that gives the oncoming main downstroke its almost singing quality. In my classes I used to insist on this singing which, by our second session, became as fully 'audible' (as I hope here visible) to beginning students.

Seeking a suitably narrow body for this running hand, Arrighi's two bottom lines show this sequence:

□ ⁓ ⌐ ⌐ a a ⌐ ⌐ d g ⁚ g □

a d c g g.

which fully establishes the slim & sloping half-square as the norm for body-width. Yet most of the headstrokes here are flat or sloping, rather than in the arc-form he uses throughout his manual & in his manuscripts. Note that the C in his bottom line ~~line~~ has a properly curved base, but a's rising passage from base is a rigid diagonal rather than an upswept narrow curve: that is, a vs. a. Comparing the two counters, the one is a crude triangle, the other a flowing contour. Yet these pointed forms must be forgiven. To cut narrow curves in a size so small was a real difficulty to the block-maker. But the edged ^pen writes them easily.

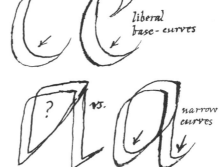

liberal base-curves

? vs.

narrow curves

The reader already understands that our italic's slim bodies can only fit into a tallish sloped oblong, & never a full square, for a square would fatten the slims into rounds. Arrighi repeats this rule, that letters should be "formed within this sloping oblong ⫽, and not within a perfect square □." But the latter phrase, in the

43

Italian "quadro perfetto □", carries, instead of the square showing what is forbidden, the sloping oblong figure instead, thus confusing the reader. My translation, therefore (perhaps for the first time), now restores the intended original meaning, namely that a bulky square remains the one enemy of the slender letter.

}Page 8{ Headstrokes for ascending characters will threaten the grace of our slim letters if the opening strokes have too much bulk. The pen starts a tiny arc downward to the right, then retraces & lengthens it leftward, creating a thin transit as it leaps downward to form the main stem. This thin transit not only reassures the hand's movement, but creates the thin relief between the firm weights leading into & out of it. This thin transit is a kind of breathing stroke which the educated nib learns to make even more effective by almost leaving the paper's surface to create the slim element a slender letter thrives upon. Even a beginner sees that if the pen is allowed, at its very start, to leap into the main downstroke, the result can only be a blunted, not a truly shaped top for all ascenders, & for a c g q as well. And note also that our k's (now unscrifed) stem is not touched by the final stroke: k k.

44

In writing the nethermost terminals of j p y and other such westbound descenders, it is at once apparent that each ends in a curve that stop directly it begins its upward course—curving just enough to tell the reading eye that it belongs with its x-height fellows just above. And the line's curved headstrokes return the compliment from above, thus confirming the (compact extenders) with their mutual x-height. Do not deform these nether terminals by angular upward bends into j p or into upward thrusts such as j j p p, & remember that p & k look their best when their final strokes just avoid contact with the stem: pk, not pk!

The crossing of t & f and of tt & ff should extend a token to the left but more to the right, the top of the crossbar coinciding with the top of the x-height. Some current manuals inadvertently show crossbars too thick, dwarfing the stems they cross. And all crossbars (including ft & tf) should be horizontals, not obliques, & not merely affixed to the right of the stem, but plainly crossed, with perhaps a tiny pen-lift at at the end, to gain a subtle expiry. The rebounds at baseline of t & tt (as also for [& [[) should be narrow, not full curves.

The promised words on the Ampersand are in order, now that the reader has met on these pages some varieties of & & ET. Each is a version of the sign of continuity which printing took over from scribal practice. Each ampersand form is logically obliged to retain some vestige of the original components *l* and *t*. Though amiably called the alphabet's 27th letter, it was no part of the Latin alphabet. It is purely a device of scriptorial days when a team of scribes, taking dictation from a chosen reader, somehow evolved this handy mark, less perhaps for space economy than as a 'breather' to relieve the rhythmic tedium of their work. Perhaps the simplest form began as a Greek alpha, ⍺, which once served for the completed mark; it soon gained a loop at the top: ⍺ + ° = &. Note that it starts with the downstroke, which may (I do not say must) take a completing serif at its top: &, whence came the single-stroke version &, again serifed as &. Then came ET ET & e⁷ EO & &c, bringing us down to date.

Some of the ampersands in the <u>Operina</u>, notably in display usage, remain a minor mystery. Arrighi himself (to judge from his manuscripts) could not have written them so clumsily; nor can Ugo da Carpi have cut them so ineptly, considering his ease with harder characters. The mystery deepens when I recall how readily every known ampersand was mastered by all my classes over many years of teaching. For ourselves, using the edged pen, it is easy to avoid any misshaping of ampersands. The & model's subtle sequence of counters almost prevents them from degenerating into ⍺ or ⍺; and in the &, no pen willingly produces &! In the ET, generously broad of

46

beam, it is easy to avoid the invidious *&* with its starved opening and its oblique finish, insulting to every honest T. We must make sure, in *&*, to keep the risen crossbar horizontal, and of modest thickness. And the spiral seduction of the 17ᵗʰ century *&* will see to its own perfection. Finally, in the late Jan van Krimpen's *&* and *&* the latter needs extra **height** to avoid cramping the loop. These two, the only contemporary forms to gain wide use, can stand comparison with the best of the past, and should be used with the care *&* gratitude their still-lively creator-spirit deserves.

⌐ Page 10 ⌐ Special care is needed to keep the hairpin arches of M *&* N angular and narrow but never spiky. This is easy if we start each in the upper half of the body height, NMN; for if the branch starts lower it creates the very sprawl that banishes all slimness. Notice how hard a time da Carpi had in some of the lower closely-packed lines where mere spikes in M make a caricature of M. This page's single novelty is the added height allowed for p *&* t's opening stems, which are to rise into the ascender area by something less than 2 nib-widths. This special privilege is shown in line 12 (the overpacked line). It will be noticed that M's arches are often set closer together than those of N, since the stoutness of M must be closely watched in a script that cannot afford to lose its general slimness.

47

ʃ To the long ʃ—an uncrossed f now long disused save in transcribing an archaic text—Arrighi now adds the smaller one, with the curves foreshortened. This S, along with its capital S, is the most ~~but~~ striking proof of the edged pen's coöperative aid. I can still recall my childhood difficulties in 'noodling out' its compound curves— difficulties I would have escaped with an edged pen. Of its two curves, the nether is the larger, but not by much— a subtlety that escapes the eager beaver intent upon S or S, when all we need is S, which begins with the familiar thick shallow arc, whose bulk declines and swells again in turning its first curve; then, entering its compound twist, it continues downward & westward, emerging at base in an equal-ly shallow curve, but longer than the top one. Now if the gracious reader will turn this book upside down, each of these grouped letters will explain (in total silence) why, in almost every so-called two-story letter, the eye wants the nether half, the nether half, to be the roomier, but not by much! Such simple tests will reduce any tendency to overdo in in dangerous places. The S-members of the Trajan inscription in Rome (dating from 114 A.D.) are early examples of this ratio of S, a letter which uniquely

sSsSsSsS

leans forward within a family of verticals.

)Page 12(The X, Y & Z are given liberal space because they cannot be cramped into a narrow oblong. The X & Y need extra leg-room, the Z Z extra head-room as well; & the double-Z, a well-exploited feature in Italian, does tend to brighten the page. Each Z is written without a pen-lift, but may freely touch or cross its twin, thus becoming a letter hard to confine: Z Z Z, & so down to a modest ZZ, or even a self-effacing zz; whence it is clear that if Z is a letter difficult to confine, X & Y are comparatively docile. Note that page 12's XaYa sequence shows only two Xamples with nether sweeps; the Y's sweep remains obligatory, whether in Y or Y.

)Page 13(This is our break-through page! All preceding pages tell us to use the 'flat and thick' headstroke to start certain letters. But now, in the upper half of the page, Arrighi tells us, for the first time, to make all ascenders equal, "as are bdhkl, with the little top leaning forward, rounded [repeat: rounded] and thick, like the beginning of cll." Rounded is what I have long thought it should be, and now we have Arrighi's own approval! I feel sure he knew this from the start, but preferred not to overburden the beginner; he knew that a tyro using an edged pen must feel, in so delicate a starting passage, that a curved opening headstroke fairly leaps into the coming mainstroke. Hence, by page 13, the beginner is ready

49

to take Arrighi's quiet hint for a change from the flat to the arc-like opening. In all my years of teaching I have insisted—as my earliest class-charts written with a felt pen at a 10" x-heig^{h}t will show—upon an opening arc rather than a flat form. In riding out this arc, the edged pen always 'remembers' to insert a thin relief-interval as it dives into the main-stroke. A flat stroke here could only blunt this headstroke, as every page in <u>Operina</u> shows, though not made explicit until page 13.

❡ In putting letters together into words, Arrighi's advice can be summarized in the phrase "optical spacing"—the placing of letter-units at separations not readily measurable, yet giving intervals of which the trained eye can accept as equal. Every normal eye, by this training, learns to judge of such equality; never, in all my teaching, has a class ever disagreed upon such equalities or inequalities.

⟩Page 14⟨ Arrighi here shows these as the only 2-stroke letters: d e f k p t x & . By now our serifless ^{k} can join the single-stroke group; and so can the ampersand he shows, if only we start it (as most others do) at upper right, all as previously shown: & & & . Also, a one-stroke alternative to his g & to our q is 2; its techni ^{ue}q can soon be applied to the arabic 9 — a numeral ^{he} did not need, having used only the roman; but we shall add the arabics later.

50

Page 15 Joining letter to letter is a problem that will largely solve itself when the scribe has learned their individual quirks, each suggesting workable solutions according to its formal needs. You will find useful a variant opening: b d h kl, avoiding the two faulty styles too usually offered in too many writing books which, I think, imprison what most needs liberation, a way of starting a letter easily rather than stiffly. The magnified forms below seem rigid,

deriving from a mitre box or a mechanical tool. They mean well, but need to think on the motto: 'withhold thy good'. I propose instead an almost

effortless, faint gliding spur, just enough to start the ink flowing into the mainstroke. It banishes the mitred-mechanical oblique by a touch of great delicacy & sure effect. ❧ *Joinability in general*, Arrighi suggests, becomes a problem only after the letter-shapes are mastered. He thus leaves to the aspiring scribe the question: To join or not to join? By that time the scribe's taste has been formed by the letters' own discipline.

51

abc + Arabics, Ligatures & Extras

rvabbbcddc+=e ffghhijkklllmnopqoq

rrrrrr sst spctuvwxyyzZZ a+°= &eeeTa &c

012 3457968 -- [("; ;")] £¢$†!!?§ *Z &c

The Arabic numerals, unconsidered by Arrighi, have here been ar-
ranged for quick structural remembrance. The sole x-height figures are
0, 1 & 2; the sole ascenders are 6 & 8; all the rest are descenders.
However, these extenders rise above, or fall below, the x-ht. by only a
scant 2 pen-widths, as the chart above shows. And note also the
dotted median line's position in 4 & 9 as compared with 6 & 8. It is
clear, too, that 6 & 9 are inverted twins. As to shaping, the 8 alone looks
difficult, but should be easy, now that we have been disciplined by the
small s. This, we recall, is made in continuous curves, ending in a stopped
arc rising from base. The 8 simply carries this base curve upward, to
merge with the starting arc at the top. To our downward passage we now
add a return upward, the sequence being S+2 = 888, making sure that
the nether counter is a bit taller and fuller than is the top. The figure 2, if
used terminally in a sum or a sentence, can lengthen its base stroke into:
2, 52, 702, 1652, 1492, &c. In shaping a 7, think of a Z
with its oblique descent southwestward. You may often see it made like

an inverted roman capital L, which never fails to surprise, as in 1977,
since it looks far better as 1977; so don't forget the Z as a corrective-in-advance!

Of the extras, the exclamation point needs some practical method of
making it a downward-pointing spike. How is this to be done with an
edged pen? By setting it at normal, with lower corner a bit above upper
limit of x-ht. ⁙ and pushing its load of ink $\frac{1}{16}$" upward; we now retrace
this downward at normal slope, thus shifting the ink downward—but
on our way down we lift the pen gradually clear of the paper, thus at=
tenuating the uppermost thickness into a vanishing thin, whose point
ends far enough above base to give clearance thereon for the period under
the wedge's spike. This is called pen management, with the scribe in charge.

} Page 16 { Because a d i k l m n u have such usefully thin
terminals, Arrighi declares them joinable to all following
letters. We have already suggested a like status for c, since it is joinable from both base & median levels. But today even b, p & s have
been joined by a thin upstroke from their bases, and the round-bottomed
b offers an additional horizontal join from its middle, the working rule being
to keep the weight of any join unobtrusive. In my working abc } P·15 {
I show a way to bring even r into the joinable group by narrowing its
wavy ending. The wider-flowing wave can still have its larky career
in terminal use, always under discretion.

The t's cross-stroke starts a natural ligature into a number of x-ht and descending letters, so that extra care is needed to keep their base-rebound curved strokes narrow, as in tt. And even without a cross-stroke problem, it is useful here to invoke alike care with ll, since a base curve springing widely will not only divide these twins but grossly over-space their word.

Ligatured forms will be best understood if we start with the familiar ff, often written ff, where disparity of height is a help. Our double ss began as an archaic long form ∬ composed *in* two identical shapes. Its better-known archaic form ß must not be allowed any middle sprawl, for obvious reasons. The same goes for ſt ſt ſt ſſ and for this series: ct ct & ſp ſp. Please note that the lateral loops are less aggressive than high-climbers such as ct ſp ſt! All are now familiar save only in point of their lateral spacing. Yet an older archaic usage permitted these so-called ligatures often to create separation as in ſt ſt ct ct, rather than union. Such sprawling forms, coming amid solid matter, create gaping holes in the page. They look far better when united by normal spacing than when divided, even by a masterly decorative ligature.

Joining V & W. The pointed V occurs usually in Arrighi's capitals, where the question of joinability does not arise; and W is not in the Italian alphabet. So for our English usage the simple horizontal join is adequate. For emergencies, experience teaches us to moderate

54

the weight of the horizontals by noting whether your pen-position
needs some slight correction to let the vertical weights properly exceed
the horizontal. This deserves some care, since the crossbar's thickness is
itself a constant & corrective check; and the scribe soon sees how de-
pendably his edged pen restores the ordained weights in critical places.

⌐Page 17⌐ Having completed his Chancery Cursive small letters,
Arrighi deals with the matter of slope. As we know from
our 19th century business hand, slope is bound to increase as we come
to write more rapidly. Indeed the business hand, starting as it did
with far greater slope than most others, often ended with characters
that fairly fell forward on their faces. Chancery Cursive asks a mere
5° to 7° forward slope from the vertical. A beginner should not unduly
exceed this slope, for his coming study of capitals will be easier if the
small letters do not seem to pull away from the opening capitals.

¶ The unique out-of-step line. Midway on his 17th page Arrighi shows
a glaringly oversloped Latin line, but fails to criticize adequately its evident
fault. As this is the only contradictory example in the entire book, a word
from the master was in order, for the reader's sake. My translation
removes all tolerance for a slope so grossly excessive…. And yet, on a page
whose remaining lines are all in the normal slope prevailing through his text,
surely a master scribe is entitled, ① to show one maverick eagerbeaverish
Latin line grossly oversloped, & ② to let posterity catch his ironical intent!

Without confessing it, Arrighi shows himself, in prac-

Page 18
tice, no stickler for the strictly-vertical capitals he recommends,
though the lapses may be da Carpi's rather than his own. But the rule for
western & near-Eastern scripts is that each should tilt in the direction of
reading—all western to the right, all near-Eastern to the left. My own practice is to slope the caps a trifle less than the text proper. When I write a
strictly vertical cap, it seems to be recoiling from its following small letter.
What disturbs me most is a cap that slopes a mere tenth of a degree
<u>backward</u> from the vertical. And since our reading direction is to the
right, I prefer a like (though merely token) direction for the cap as well.
Where the prevailing rhythm is forward-to-the-right, a strict vertical cap
is under constant risk of slippage further backward. A single such
lapse disturbs that rhythm and draws unwanted attention to its
offense. So, if the scribe will merely keep his cap-slope, however
slight, on the safer right side of the vertical, no eye will be disaffected,
and his page's dignity will moult no feather.

Page 19
If we allow the usual 5 nib-widths of the pen-in-hand to
constitute our x-ht. (meaning body-height), we must also
allow, as Arrighi's every page shows, a white band of equal height to con-
tain the risers and descenders of every such line. Naturally, any over-
running of extender heights or depths of letters will risk collisions between a descender of one line & an ascender of the next. Arrighi's rules

for letter- and word-spacing in each line are simple, & will soon set up
a working logic of their own.

What the beginner needs
⟩Page 20⟨ (and is shown alongside) is
a set of simple roman skeletons derived from
the famous Trajan forms on open-air view
in Rome since 114 A·D. Incised in six lines
on a marble slab 9 feet long by 4 feet high,
set upon the pedestal of its 70-foot column,
                    written on the stone
the inscription was (before it was cut) in

Skeleton Forms Developed
from Trajan Inscription

Full Square	½ Sq.	3/4 Square	
□	B	C	A
M	E	G	X
W	F	D	K
⅓ Sq. at most	L	O	R
I	P	Q	Y
J	S	V	Z

letters of such clarity & grace as to deserve their kindly treatment by time
& the elements. The writing tool, essentially like our own, was a broad-
edged brush some 5/8" wide, its "pen angle" generally 15°, but flattened
to 8° for O & Q, and steepened for certain angular forms. The above
chart roughly classifies them by body-widths, so that the italic writer
may learn discretion in the sweeps or flourishes they demand. When, on
his 7ᵗʰ page, Arrighi offered the slim oblong as the ideal shape to con-
tain the Chancery Cursive small letter, he forgot to say that for its caps
we shall be reverting to the square & circle, which had helped to fix
their proportions. These are now shown in simple form, very
slightly forward in slope, at the allowed cap-height of 7½ nib-widths.
All follow the Trajan family's breadth formula of our preceding chart

in being as varied, & yet as subtly unified, as siblings tend to be:

ABCDEF GHIJKLM N
OPQRSTUVWXYZ &c.

The forms are spare enough, but there is added comfort in our edged pen's 'remembering' to differentiate the strong southeastward diagonals from the less-strong uprights & the least-strong northeastward thin strokes. We note that I & J each fill barely ⅛ of the square, M & W each need a whole square; B E F L P S each fill ½ the square, & C D G O Q · A H K R T U U V X Y Z each fill ¾ to ⅞ of the square. B's nether counter is a bit deeper & broader than the upper, yet their combined area comes to just half the square. Both R & K have narow upper counters, gaining width by a generous spread at base. M & W are inversely related; each is a full square in area, but W's paired apexes are a bit pinched together whereas M's are wider apart. In both letters the large middle angle is flanked by twins of lesser spread, and no two lines in either letter are parallel.

Pages 21-32 When you are familiar with the simple roman caps, their writing in Italic trim becomes, as Arrighi promises, an easy matter. We already know their allowance of 7½ p-w. for height. But as you become confident in their shaping you may well find yourself preferring a height of 7 or even 6 p-w. Learn all the variant cap-forms on pages 22 to 32. All will be useful in your transcriptions, whether of Arrighi's practice texts in the given Latin or Italian, or better still, as I have suggested, if you use such short texts you have gathered in English French, German, Italian or other Continental tongues. All will, in Arrighi's phrase, serve "for training the hand." They will open new vistas, especially if the scribe has the courage to subdue his cap-height from 7½ p-w. to 7, to 6½, even to 6, & meanwhile look intently at Arrighi's techniques of cap-subdual on his _Operina pages_.

℔ As to C & C. There is a too-common fashion of starving the capital C into C, which insults its classic origin, which accorded a fuller-bodied stability. The starved form deserves retirement because it competes with the venerable 'hanging' C, whose main function it is to house in its basement a following x-ht. letter. This should be so aligned as to bisect the tenant's bulk, with more white space showing below than above the resident vowel: Cā Cē Cī Cō Cū. Nor should this C normally extend more than 4 p-w. below baseline. We have altogether too many examples (often, alas! historic, beginning in the mid-1500's) of a double-faulted C which seems either ① to be seeking extra tenants for its basement, or ② stiffening its back from a gentle curve into a rigid vertical.

℔ As to the hanging G. Line 1 of the manual's page 21 shows a version of this letter just twice as tall and only half as broad, with a droopy middle serif reaching & almost touching the back. Perhaps we should learn to think of both C & G as invasion-prone, the C by over-sized mislocated tenants, the G by needless serifs. Is G improved by being made into G or G? Many years ago a book from abroad offered an italic G whose baroque serifs took full command. It is shown here only to fore-stall such well-meaning prettification as may even now be aborning.

The hanging C & G are in a sense twin letters, as → C G G may suggest. Each opens with an upper ᵃʳᶜ which curves slightly (never straightens) in descent: G C G C C G

⁕ As to K & R. These are twins of a sort, each body narrow of top, spreading at bottom, & each vastly improved by avoiding con-tact with opening stem. K & R thus produce an expiring sweep of tail ideally suited to a cursive script. The archaic R & K persisted briefly, but have yielded to R & K

⁕ As to B D & P P R R. Every capital Arrighi offers has its uses. But since many are meant for design or decorative problems, I suggest some forms for everyday ᵘˢᵉ with remarks upon their making. All in this group start with a downward stem, ending thus for the first two: L L B D ꞊D; the remaining four letters differ thus at base: IJ, IJ, P P, R R. But all these share a common over-arching by a mush-room-shaped top which must never be flattened. If you can write this arc without touching (but just clearing) the top of the stem, the tiny shaft

60

of white light so gained will illumine not only these four letters but show the merit of a like treatment in E F T's horizontal sweeps as well. And if B P R's upper counters can avoid a mid-stem touch by their descending curves, you will see a new value in <u>unflooded</u> passages of this kind. Note also that the upper counters end <u>not</u> midway in the letters' height but— as in K— visibly and subtly a hair's breadth above. Returning to the rounded opening sweeps, instruction-by-contrast is in order. Look at this shrunken sequence of mushroom-rising curves in B D P R and see how they impoverish what ought to be free-swinging & generous. An even more gruesome flat-top version of these— B D P R— will teach us what to avoid! But with an opening fullness restored, B D P R regain the running-hand look.

¶ As to <u>Horizontal Sweeps</u>. Sweeps usually start about halfway up the cap-height, their width roughly scaled to the letter's body-breadth. A narrow sweep can only produce (except in I or J) a huddled, cramped letter. Almost all will benefit by generosity, as these contrasts will show:

A A E E E F F H H K K M M
N N T T U U V V W W

For E, a ½ sq. in the roman, I have used & taught a widened stabilized form better shown as E, whence E; & for L, ½ sq., La La, whence La La, all now ready for use.

❦ Cap A's Opening Downstroke. Italic A often tempts the beginner into excess by a delusion of 'equal treatment'— that is, to keep its two convergent stems essentially straight. This is correct when it is a roman cap, but a running italic needs more evident flow. Roman A, being in the full-bodied class, has ample spread in its square. But in its italic use a single straight wall (the second) A A A is all it can endure; and each letter alongside duly shows that second wall unchanged. Now A A A look at the upper line's rigid opening down-stroke: it travels straight southwest, with a short arc at the end. Look now at the nether figures: each descending first wall is bowed from beginning to end, whence we get   A A A , functioning much as it does in the M & admitting it to membership in the Italic family

❦ Horizontal Serifs. We know I & J, and in learning I & J our great care will be to keep the serifs to a modest weight. At our 45° pen-position the horizontal serif too often seems aggressive, so we must reduce its bulk by flattening slightly our pen-position. We must remember that it is not weight but definition that makes a serif effective. Try these extremes III, III, and then make your choice of optimum serif weights. I speak here only of horizon-tal serifs. Vertical serifs, because of their diminutive size, their delicacy & technical difficulty, must wait until our scribe is a solid practitioner.

¶ Tails for Q Y Z. These are caps already so graceful as to need little further decoration. Q's tail in Italic script should not be corrupted by compound curves such as Q; nor does Z or Z improve by becoming Z. There is a one-stroke Q that came alive to me (as doubtless to others) while writing number 9; out of it grew Q, provided that my "9" carried its curvature below base; if it lapsed into Q the result was too rigid, until I wrote it as Q. Speaking of tails, Arrighi has been generous with decorative openings and endings for his capitals, including X, Y Z, but has overlooked a base-serifed form for Y when, as often happens in a cap-grouping, too many caps are competing for notice. So, I offer a reasonably oldish alternative that ends on baseline, a kind of ram's-horn Y made to order for the edged pen: Y Y Y. Note that the horns are of equal height & breadth, supported by a stem unencumbered by their weight.

¶ Reaching the Z. Early italic scribes created the Z as almost a linguistic monopoly— one that English can share, if we can avoid the razzle-dazzle. Usage now permits either z to cross its twin, provided air enough is left for both z's to breathe.

A Note on Speed
& on the Use of Italic Anthologies

The beginner, for whom the foregoing pages were written, is already (having read them) no longer a simon-pure beginner. Indeed, he may be more judgmatical than most readers of the past, chiefly because Stanley Morison's 1926 <u>Operina</u> facsimile (with its evaluative essay on Arrighi's work) has deepened every layman's knowledge of handwriting's history.

My gracious reader now understands that no handwriting can run before it has learned to walk. In forming the letters he realizes how much he owes to the edged pen. This rediscovered tool will subtly teach far more than he can have expected. I say more because the pressure for mere speed in writing is today virtually banished by the electric typewriter, which has set the hand free at last to cultivate quality again. Arrighi's hand can again serve society even if his running hand begins as a jogging hand.

The scribe begins, I say, by teaching the pen a leisured walk, and as italic is equipped for joinability, he senses the quiet stimulus of the running alphabet. He steadily gains the rhythmic quality such flowing forms induce. In fact, each incipient awkwardness often suggests its own cure by exercises the scribe both devises and performs, with a discrimination that makes him in good part his own teacher.

I therefore list below a few publications containing showings of Chancery Cursive writings by past & present scribes – each a worthy exemplar. Together they form a gallery of efforts by fellow-strivers in the italic hand from the Renaissance to our own time. All are published in England, but can be found here in bookshops, art-supply shops and libraries.

① Alfred Fairbank. _A Book of Scripts._ Penguin Books. Revisions have brought this popular showing of historic scripts from 48 plates in 1949 to 80 plates in the 1977 edition.

② A.J. Fairbank & R.W. Hunt. _Humanistic Script of the XV & XVI Centuries._ Oxford University Press. 1976. A pamphlet of 24 examples chosen from Mss. in the Bodleian Library.

③ Wilfred Blunt. _Sweet Roman Hand._ 1952. Lively present-day examples in the Italic Hand (which was called 'Roman' by Shakespeare in "Twelfth Night").

④ Wilfred Blunt & Will Carter. _Italic Handwriting. Some Examples_ [total, 43] _of Everyday Cursive Hands._ 1954.

⑤ Alfred Fairbank & Berthold Wolpe. _Renaissance Handwriting: An Anthology of Italic Scripts._ 1960.

Of the above, number 5 has the widest range, showing (with sympathetic commentary) 110 examples from italic's very beginning. Only the last eight plates show writings of the present century. Numbers 3 & 4 are confined to contemporary italic writing, each of course revealing in some degree the influence of earlier masters.

66

Today's students will find these appealing in a special way, since each example has been written at a time and under pressures we all understand by having shared. And each will reveal, or at least intimate, responses in taste and temperament very like our own as we in our turn now set about recapturing this stately & vigorous handwriting.

L.S.